Chased by your Grace

Mikael RÉALE

Illustration: Vraiment Libre Entraide & Développement
© 2015 Mikael RÉALE/VLED

Edition : BoD - Books on Demand
12/14 Rond-point des Champs Élysées
75008 Paris
Printed by BoD – Books on Demand, Norderstedt

ISBN: 9782322043118
Dépôt légal: November 2015

For all those who seek…

Forward
by Lee Lacoss

In these times, the voice of God is shaking heaven and earth. He has promised that, "Once more I shake not only the earth, but also heaven." (Hebrews 12:25-29) By proclaiming that He will do this 'once more,' He indicates that this will involve the removal of all those things that are being shaken. That which can be shaken are the things that are made or manufactured. On the other hand, the things which cannot be shaken will remain. The writer of these scriptures goes on to say, "Therefore, since we are receiving a kingdom which cannot be shaken, let us have grace, by which we may serve God acceptably with reverence and godly fear." So, whatever is not of the kingdom of God is 'made' or manufactured; and with His voice, God will so shake all those things to the point of their removal. Only that which is created by God, according to His Word, will endure this shaking process. That's the point, isn't it? There is so much in the earth (and, according to the Lord, also in heaven) that is not created by Him. He creates and upholds all things by His powerful Word. Therefore, God promised there would be a time, and it is now, when He will rid heaven and earth of all that is not created. That is, also by His voice, He will eliminate all that is not a result of, and/or in agreement with, His will, which is expressed by His Word.

We are admonished and encouraged to have 'grace.' It is only with His grace that one can serve God acceptably—with reverence and godly fear, or with worshipful honor. Grace is the key. Grace is the way, the only way, to serve Him acceptably. In these days, we are faced with the same deceptions and false doctrines that the early church encountered. At that time, in order to have the light of God's truth dispel the encroaching darkness, the apostles and elders met in Jerusalem. They had to contend with those false doctrines that were putting a yoke of bondage upon the disciples, which Peter says neither the Jews that were present, nor their fathers, were able to bear. This apostle says that all such attempts, to have one saved by a mixture of grace and self-justification by attempting to keep the law, actually tempts God." (Acts 15:1-16) Today, we hear of, and are faced with, the same attempts to burden Jesus' disciples. All such efforts simultaneously tempt God, Himself. In our weaknesses, in our temptations, in our afflictions, in all things, He says, "My grace is sufficient."

Another apostle, Paul by name, tells us that He, the Lord, has predestined us to adoption as sons, according to His good pleasure. This is to the praise of the "glory of His grace." (Eph. 1:4-6) God's glory is inextricably united with His grace. And, we remember that one called Haggai, a prophet, said that when God shakes all things, He will fill His house with glory. (Hag. 2:6-8) As we learn more about His grace with Mikael, may we, who are His dwelling place, be further filled with His glory. May the glory of His grace fill the earth, as He so desires.

There is hope and there is the way, His way. He is the way. This book is more than words on a page. His word is spirit and life. Life is seen and experienced as we allow His word to feed and inspire us through the pages of this journey.

Mikael has so clearly taken hold of this reality. With great passion that has grown out of revelation and much personal experience and inspired reflection, he lives out before us many facets of what is, and what is not, grace.

Our prayer is quite simple, yet life-changing:

"Father, we do not want to fall short of the glory of the Lord. We desire to behold the glory of the Lord, and to be changed into

His image from glory to glory. Lord, as if looking into a mirror, help us to see clearly so there is no veil over our face, mind or heart by trying to come to You through our legalistic works. We thank You that any and all such veils are taken away in Christ. With the prophet, we cry, "Grace, Grace to the cornerstone, which is Christ, the Head, and to the temple, which is Christ, His Body."

Lee LaCoss

PROLOGUE

Meeting at the end of the world!

I was born in 1963 in Lyon, France, into a well-to-do family. Westerners from North Africa, known in France as "Pieds-noirs," that is, 'black feet.'

These origins had a lot of influence on my education and also gave me the feeling of being constantly uprooted, a feeling that has been impossible to erase and which still exists within me today. This was reinforced at the age of 18 months, when I was left in the care of my maternal grandparents until 1969. It was then that my father was transferred to St. Raphael, nearby in southern France.

In the years that followed rebellious feelings grew within me. I dreamt of nothing but travel and boats and islands. One day after an intense father-son wrangling, I felt that I had been particularly unjustly treated. I resolved to leave, and hid aboard a cargo ship at Tahiti, where my father was posted at the time. I was 15. Six days later a plane from COTAM (an airline reserved for French military personnel) took me back to Tahiti to be with my parents. Although I was with my family for a while, I had nonetheless caught the 'virus' of the sea and liberty, and it was now in my blood forever.

One year later, when we had come home to France, I left again, just two weeks before my seventeenth birthday. This time they didn't bring me back. I made a living through music and mime in the streets, and in cafes and restaurants.

It was at this time that the army came for me: conscription was still a legal obligation in France! For me it was evident that this would be a waste of a year. And, anyway, as Boris VIAN, a French poet, said, 'Mr. President, I wasn't put on this earth to kill people.'

On the other hand, I considered my father's orders to be unwarranted, too. It wasn't an 'upstart from a higher rank' who was going to tell me what to do! It was decided that I would desert. I sold my car to buy a oneway ticket to New York and arrived with 137 US dollars in my pocket. Not speaking a word of English, I began to tag along with a group of Haitians from Greenwich Village. I was put up by a homosexual who had lived in France, who taught me the rudiments of the American language.

After some time in New York the cold of an early winter pushed me towards the south, and several weeks later I arrived in California. I had always been a bit of a "Troubadour," but was becoming more and more of a schemer. "By chance," I was expelled from the states a year later, for not having a valid visa. I had begun to get involved in more dangerous games, like falsifying travelers checks and drug trafficking. Consequently, I tasted the Californian prison system for a week. I thank God today for taking me out of all this without any lasting stain or being destroyed by drugs.

I crossed the South Pacific to Polynesia. I had been thinking of setting up myself there some years earlier. I had promised myself to return to Polynesia after having lived there with my parents and then left the island to return to city life. The only problem on returning to this, the country of my dreams, was that my father had tipped off the local police that I had refused my military call-up. He told them that they could find me on the island of Moorea. This was French territory so I had a visit from the police in the following days.

There was the prospect of a return to France with barracks at the end of the journey, but for me this was out of the question. With the airport officials on the lookout for me, the police decided that I couldn't get out of the territory, so they didn't bother trying to capture me. Being a sailing instructor, it wasn't difficult for me to find an American sailing ship which was looking for a team to cross the Pacific to New Zealand and so I left Moorea secretly.

Once again, my life was filled with music and schemes, but in this small country which is socially exceptionally stable, this would prove to be more difficult to get by than doing such things in California. However, this was how the most extraordinary event in my life came about. In Auckland, I met a young guy from Quebec, who was also travelling. I invited him to spend the night at the place where my friends had put me up, since they were out for the evening. That evening he told me about his journey. He had been living with friends in a big white house on a surf beach. There was an old red surf board nailed to the front of it… a dream or what! But the thing that surprised me the most was when he told me that a month before, he had become a Christian.

For my part, apart from eight years of catechism that I had been involved with in my childhood, my only other contacts with "Christians" were these Jesus freaks (fanatics for Jesus) that had often encountered me in the USA. I had never completely understood them. This guy spoke to me with great simplicity, and at the same time with great faith in this Jesus. This Biblical character from my childhood was becoming more and more real. Towards midnight, I was worn out and went to bed. In the morning, when I got up, I discovered that he had gone. On the bedside table, he had left a note with his address in New Zealand, and a request for mine. He had added, "Never forget Mikael, Jesus loves you." It was because of this note that the most incredible episode of all my travels was about to start.

Three days after the meeting with this lad (he was called Fred), my heart was boiling with one desire—to see him again before my return to France. I refused to admit to myself that I wanted to hear more on the subject of Jesus. The "official reason" that I gave to my friends, and to myself, was "the surf."

So I took my bag and my guitar and I left Auckland for the address that he had given me. After two or three hours of hitch-hiking, I arrived in the village. I went to the address, but a major disappointment awaited me. Fred didn't live there. It was only a postal address, and he had not been there for two or three weeks. No one knew where he could be found or where the white house on the surfing beach was. On top of this, this village was more than 100 km from the nearest beach.

I decided to return to Auckland, but the first car that picked me up was going towards the east coast. Before I realised it, I was a long way from my return route.

Never mind, I had the time. I wanted to go surfing and above all, I was "free!" During all my years of hitch-hiking things had never gone so well. And a few hours later, we arrived at the fantastic beaches of the South Pacific. We arrived at a pub and I suggested to my "driver" that we stop for a beer, but he was pressed for time, and so he left me there. As I was about to cross the road I looked right and then left and then ahead… and there, in front of me, was a large white house. On the front of which an old Hawaiian surf board was stuck. A red surf board!

I was taken aback. I crossed the lawn slowly, and it was with a trembling hand that I knocked on the door. A big blond guy with an Australian accent answered the door. I asked him, hesitantly, if a man named, Fred, from Quebec, lived there. "I'll call him for you," he said. And two minutes later, I found myself face to face with him. "Hey! Mikael!" said Fred, "This is great, we've been praying for three days for you to come." I desperately tried to make him understand that I was there for the surf, but I didn't know where I was. How was all of this possible?

The days that followed were interspersed with surfing, music and discussions on all sorts of subjects and in particular about me.

The guys who lived there seemed as if they were really interested in me personally; and they also spoke of this Jesus, as though they knew him personally. The problem for me was that my family had made me practice this religion in a really intensive way since the age of eight. I had served at mass and I had been "The Little Singer at the Wooden Cross."

I had also sung in front of the Pope in 1975 at Christmas. I had continued to present myself at the chaplaincy for two years after my communion. So this God was someone that I had heard more than enough about! For me, he was nothing more than a tyrant, thirsty for riches in a world of people dying of hunger. Certainly God existed, but he couldn't be the one represented by the Christians. I had read the gospels, and the Jesus of these books was so different from the "Christians' version" that it seemed to me, to be honest, he must have long since quit Christianity. Another thing bothered me, the ease with which one could affirm one's faith. "I am a Christian" say "yes" to Jesus, "I am a sinner. I need You. I give you my life." This seemed too easy! In any case, I was no more a sinner than anyone else, and if this truly was the case, it was because life had not given me any other choice.

Nevertheless, one evening, this was all going to change.

I had been asleep for half an hour when I sensed a horrible presence at my side. A sort of monster seemed to be hiding there in the dark, ready to leap on me. Like a terrified child, I hid myself under the covers. But I knew that this presence was there in the bed with me, and for a good reason. This horrible thing was me! I felt so nasty, so damaged, so empty. Where was my justice? I was so full of anguish, that I cried out to God!

"Listen! I don't know if you exist, I don't know if you are really called, 'Jesus,' but if everything they say about you is true, do something for me straight away!" I was overcome by a peace that I had never previously known! Every trace of anguish had disappeared and the emptiness had been replaced by an enthusiasm for life.

   I got up immediately to go and see my host in his room to tell him what I had just experienced. This didn't seem to surprise him, particularly. He simply responded to the mass of questions that I asked him. I was baptized on the surfing beach that God had allowed me to discover just four days earlier.

Baptized in Fire

Several days after these events, I took the plane to return to Europe. I was like many young converts, full of enthusiasm but clumsy. I had the ardent desire to witness about the marvelous things that had happened to me. I believed that my father, my mother, my brother and my sister, and all my friends should give their lives to Christ. Where would they be otherwise? I imagined myself taking the good news to the whole continent, ignorant of the fact that there were already Christians in France.

My mother responded to me with a vague, "that's nice." My father gave me a little smile and spoke to me about the Freemasons, whom he had just joined. My brother and sister said nothing and my friends made fun of me saying, "that doesn't surprise us about you."

It's true that the various moments I decided to share with them could have been better chosen. A week before my return to France, my father had left the family home and everyone was in a state of shock. It was as if my great enthusiasm as a young convert was melting like snow in the sun. I felt as if I was the only Christian in France. Little by little, I began to stop witnessing my faith, and I returned to the world that I had left so recently.

I spent my time playing music with a friend with whom I had gone to live. We practiced a lot to be ready for the summer season, playing in restaurants.

At the end of the summer I found myself in debt again and angry! Angry with my parents who wanted to involve me in their divorce, and angry with myself because I really had the feeling that I was spoiling everything around me.

I decided to leave the coast for the Haut Var, inland, where I could set myself up in an abandoned shepherd's hut in the hills. There was no running water or electricity, but it was fine for me after the crowds on the Cote d'Azur. I began to realize that I was losing what I had received six months earlier in New Zealand.

I remembered my Bible, opened it and read a passage about prayer. I started to pray, thinking that it was really a shame not to be able to live what was written in the passage. Suddenly, I was overcome by the same peace that I had experienced on the day of my conversion. I was isolated from every other Christian, and God had to come to me, all the same! What a marvelous discovery I made that day! I was able, yes me, Mikael, to call Jesus and he had come.

Three months later, Fred, the lad from Quebec, joined me after spending six months in a bible college in Singapore. We were happy to see each other, but at the same time we noticed there was a difference between us, spiritually. He had been in an evangelical church where he had studied since his conversion. But, as for me, I had moved forward on my own, and perhaps in a crooked way.

The following Sunday, Fred was looking for a church because he could not believe that there wasn't one in France! He found a worship group. I jumped for joy. I wasn't the only Christian in France! I simply hadn't been looking hard enough. Plus, I had felt God's presence really strongly, even during the time when the people were talking and talking. How could this be? I asked Fred to explain this to me. He spoke to me of the Day of Pentecost in the early church, and of the "baptism of the Holy Spirit." Then, he told me to read my bible, chapters 12, 13 and 14 of the first letter of St Paul to the Corinthians.

The advantage that I was able to find from not having been taught during the first months following my conversion was that I had no preconceived ideas. I had not been exposed to any church debates on the subject of the Holy Spirit.

After having read the texts that Fred had drawn to my attention, I came to the conclusion that the best thing to do was to follow the advice of the Apostle Paul, that is, to ask for the best spiritual gifts. I asked the Lord for the baptism in the Holy Spirit. Fred laid his hands on me as the Apostles had done in their time. Nothing in particular happened—and that disappointed me a lot. A few days later, though, I heard the voice of God for the first time.

It all began with the urgent need to go and see some friends living at Draguignan, fifteen kilometers away in the mountains. I left at two in the afternoon, hitchhiking, after having warned them that I was coming. Leaving the town, I put out my thumb to passing cars. I heard a voice which told me to walk and pray. The first thing that came to mind was the warmth of early spring and the fifteen kilometers that separated me from my friends, when suddenly I asked myself who had spoken to me. I refused to obey three times before understanding that something strange was happening. I walked and prayed for three hours without feeling the least bit tired. The more the kilometers passed, the more I felt the presence of God and the more I lengthened my steps. I really had the sensation of sharing my heart with God, as I would with a close friend. I had almost arrived when I suddenly stopped. The sun was ablaze on the horizon, but a bigger fire was burning within me. I felt God was very close. This lasted for about ten minutes when I heard the voice again, telling me to go! I got underway again to cover the kilometer of undergrowth that now separated me from my friends' house. Arriving in front of their house, I noticed several strange things! The Holy Spirit showed me a cloud of darkness which covered the house. I was able witness to these people, both parents and children, who were depressed. A few days later they called me to say that my visit had lifted them. The father confided in me that during the day of my arrival, he had decided he would kill the whole family and then commit suicide himself! As a result of my being with them, however, he not carry out his terrible plan.

After that day with that family, while Fred and I were seeking God's face, suddenly, quietly and then louder and louder, I began to speak in an unknown language, praising the Lord.

One Night, a Dream

If all these experiences had given me a better knowledge of my God, they had not necessarily persuaded me to follow him. Sure, I had been baptized in the Holy Spirit, but I continued to live life as it suited me. I had an attitude of rebellion, particularly where the authority of pastors was concerned at the churches that I frequented. Also, I couldn't understand that God had a say in the direction I was planning for my life. However, it was evident that my conscience, renewed by my encounter with Christ, had changed my values. Many things that seemed natural before, apparently, did not have a place in my new life. I had gotten rid of a great number of them without any problem. But, in asking Jesus to come into my life, I had invited him to come along as a passenger rather than as the driver. For me, it was as if God should only help me in what I wanted to do.

It is true that God has never abandoned me. I know today that He doesn't help us in the way that we expect. This is all more than true if we depart from the plan that He has for us. Some time after my "baptism of fire," I had met a young girl, Cathy, who I fell instantly in love with. After talking to her about Jesus, she converted and I very quickly had the conviction that she was the wife that God had planned for me. Some months later we were married at Chambery. Then we decided to go travelling in September, 1986.

I felt confused at this time because some things were not working in my relationship with God. I found it hard to pray, to read my bible, and to look like "a Christian." I was persuaded to return to the source, and my opinion was that the source was at the other end of the world. We left ten months later on a Martinique sailing boat. Our plan wasn't to go to Australia, as was originally decided, but to Quebec, to see Fred, who had also married.

After a brief time with him in Montreal, Cathy and I left for the north where we would rapidly make more new friends. I found a very good-paying job, working for the forestry department. After two months of working hard, we started to think about continuing our journey towards Australia.

During this time Cathy had been staying in the house of some friends. In the calm of North Quebec, she had gently renewed her relationship with the Lord. She had asked him to show us a local Christian fellowship, and the Holy Spirit had pointed us towards a small, new church. As for me who was working in the middle of a forest in a team of lumberjacks, I felt my faith slowly disappearing. On my return, though, I was full of enthusiasm when Cathy asked me to meet the people who had supported her during my absence. They invited me to witness at a Christian café, which they had opened in their village. And, some time later, for the first time, I lead the time of praise in a church meeting.

My spiritual life felt like it was going again, and I understood how I had been stupid to abandon meeting with Christian brothers for so long. It was great to come back, to eat, pray and evangelize together. The Lord was at work and I wanted to be in His presence. So it was that for the first time in my life that I had a dream, that is to say, a dream inspired by the Holy Spirit. This was it:

I was in the immense plains of the USA, a sprawling desert like you see in the "Westerns!" The sun going down in the distance like on a cinema screen. I was surrounded by a crowd of people, cheering me and carrying me in triumph because I was going to die for them. We were walking with the victory chants ringing in our ears, towards a kind of immense scaffolding several hundred yards high, rising towards the sky, incongruous in these surroundings. I suddenly understood that it was the tool of my approaching death, and I felt a rush of anguish. But the chants of the crowd around me and the confidence of all these people soon chased away the feeling. Then we were at the base of this construction which was made of metal tubes and wooden platforms. Between the platforms there were spiral staircases. Amongst the thousands of people who were accompanying me, a hundred or so started to climb up the stairs with me, while the others continued to cheer me upward with chants and songs. We were soon on the first level on a huge platform. The chants from the crowd could still be heard, and I felt a certain pride in that the chants were for me. After a moment, I started towards the second level, but the structure became narrower as it ascended. There were no more than about fifteen of us left able to go on. Little by little as we climbed, the noise of the crowd became blurred. When we arrived at the second level, we couldn't hear a thing. Some of those who had climbed up with me, started to go back down. The others who were still with me encouraged me one last time and I continued my climb, alone. After the first few steps a doubt crept upon me. I turned around, but there was no one there. I was alone, to climb toward my death. But what for? Why must I die for these people whom I didn't even know? Each footstep gave me a new flush of anguish and each stair felt like a mountain. A terrible fear overtook me. I began to cry, then to scream… And I woke up covered in sweat!

I thank the Lord for not making me follow this dream any longer! I know that what I was about to live through in my dream was the beginning of the passion of Christ. After sensing just a few minutes of the twenty hours of the passion of Christ, I began to understand the price that Jesus had voluntarily accepted to pay for me. We often think of the atrocious pain, the whip lashes, the humiliation of the crown of thorns, of the suffering and the agony on the cross. But there is another suffering that can be added to all the others this is having freely chosen to suffer!

This choice could not have been easy, particularly when you think that his disciples disowned him and the very people for whom he was dying, were mocking him. The choice was even more difficult when Satan's hordes surrounded him at Golgotha to try to divert him from his sacrifice. Jesus went right to the bitter end; and it would have been the same if he had only had me to save. From now on, would I still be able to waste my life? Of course not, things must change! I would no longer be able to be content with myself just being a believer. I had to become a preacher of this grace of our God!

"The Spirit of the Lord is on me because he has anointed me to preach good news to the poor; he has sent me to heal the brokenhearted and to announce that captives shall be released and the blind shall see, that the downtrodden shall be freed from their oppressors, and that God is ready to give blessings to all who come to him." (Luke 4:18-19)

But fifteen years later, I still hadn't understood the essentials of this verse in the face of the realities of my life. I still tried to justify myself in the eyes of God in many different ways.

In fact, being confronted with all of my sins, which were accumulating before my eyes, I didn't understand how God was able to put up with me. I regularly tried to please him, and often my good intentions were rewarded with failure. I was unable to accept these failures. I tried to plead my cause. The poor excuses followed: "...It's my past. I've suffered too much. It is not entirely my fault…"

I felt grace needed a little push, to convince God to give me another chance. This lasted until the day a bible text completely shook my reasoning, just as I was trying again to explain to God that I had fallen, but that it wasn't my fault.

"What happiness for those whose guilt has been forgiven! What joys when sins are covered over! What relief for those who have confessed their sins and God has cleared their record. There was a time when I wouldn't admit what a sinner I was. But my dishonesty made me miserable and filled my days with frustration. All day and all night your hand was heavy on me. My strength evaporated like water on a sunny day until I finally admitted all my sins to you and stopped trying to hide them. I said to myself, 'I will confess them to the Lord'. And you forgave me! All my guilt is gone." (Psalm 32:2-5)

This passage makes me question myself. It asks me to search to the bottom of my heart. Wouldn't I admit what a sinner I was? Was I honest?

Until I accepted, or recognized, my sins, "I wouldn't admit what a sinner I was." This would make God a liar! It is He Alone Who can say what is bad and what is good, just or unjust, true or false!

This can also lead you to a wrong type of faith that defies the truth, because it is not founded on the truth of the word of God. "I have gone too far, God is not able to love me…"

Many people proclaim the sort of things that you do not find in the word of God, and place their faith on their theology more than the biblical reality. They say, "God loves me, yes but…"

In these two cases of "untrue faith," we often find ourselves confronted by a bad perception of the character of God; and this is because we need a new revelation of the grace of God.

PART 1

THE REVELATION OF GRACE!

We have often heard, read and thought that our faith alone is the source of our salvation. I would love it if we could all study together what the bible has to say on the subject, in order that this affirmation should be based on the Word of God. We are able to clearly see what God has done for our salvation. In fact, our faith will not be truly effective unless we have received a revelation of what the grace of God is! And here's a thought that may surprise a number of us.

For years we, and those who have gone before us in faith, have imagined the following chronology concerning the spiritual history of mankind.

In the beginning, God created a perfect world, free from all sin. Adam and Eve were living in bliss in a perfect garden. Then came the fall, and the Devil corrupted God's perfect plan.

Then came the law brought by Moses, this made man aware of his position of having fallen. Finally came the grace that saved us. Jesus on the cross at Calvary—Help from God for us who are incapable of living according to the laws that He had given us.

Nevertheless, I think that it is interesting to review the "classic" view of this chronology, taking into account that the bible clearly tells us that before the creation of the world, and therefore before the fall of man, and before the law, God had already made grace available!

This appears to me today to be so important, because the understanding of this point brings us to realize that the source of our salvation is not our faith, but the unconditional love of God!

Even before the fall, the Grace!

"If you will stir up this inner power you will never be afraid to tell others about our Lord, or to let them know that I am your friend even though I am here in jail for Christ's sake. You will be ready to suffer with me for the Lord, for he will give you strength in suffering.

It is he who saved us and chose us for his holy work, not because we deserved it but because that was his plan long before the world began—to show his love and kindness to us through Christ. And now he has made all of this plain to us by the coming of our savior Jesus Christ, who broke the power of death and showed us the way of everlasting life through trusting him." (2 Timothy 1:8–10)

We see in this first text that Paul tells us that "grace had been given to us before time," and that this grace was manifested in our time by the arrival of Jesus Christ.

This first text clearly indicates to us that Jesus had not brought grace with his death on the cross, but that he had simply manifested it. This fact is reinforced by a second text, "And inhabitants of the earth will worship the beast–all whose names have not been written in the book of life belonging to the Lamb, that was slain before the creation of the world." (Revelations 13:8)

This second verse teaches us a lot. Firstly, it confirms what we have said about grace pre- existing, adding that the Lamb had been sacrificed from the foundation of the world. The biblical text is clear, the buying back of sin by the sacrifice of the Lamb happened before man even existed.

We can see, therefore, that the sacrifice of Isaac (Genesis 22) and the sacrifice of the Passover Lamb originated by Moses (Exodus 12), are not prophecies of the cross but, witnesses to the grace that God has given since the foundation of the world! Halleluiah!

The second teaching that this marvelous text gives us concerns the second doctrinal point which was lost on me for years, as with many before me, too!

Rereading this part of the text: "all whose names have not been written..." We must note before going any further that the Greek term 'ook' translated by the negative "not" can also be translated by the term "no longer."

This puts a new light on the text. Those who have chosen Satan's camp by receiving the mark of the "beast" have their name taken out of the book of the Lamb! This means that the names of those who do not receive this mark, just the same as the names of those who accept it, have been written in the book of life before the foundation of the world, but that certain of them will be taken out.

Therefore, we don't write our name in the book of life when we are born again! It has already been written there since the foundation of the world and it will stay there until our death, if we are not one of those who receive the mark of the beast.

At the moment of our physical death, if we have not accepted Jesus, it is rubbed out.

It is by putting things back in this order that we realize that God is just! Above all we realize that the principal of grace was already in the Old Testament!

This often relieves us of those obstructive questions that are often posed. "Why has God not made grace available earlier? What will happen to those who have died before Jesus died for us, or to those who have never heard the Word? etc. ..."

Then we finally come to realize that...

THE GOSPEL IS GOOD NEWS!

Definition: GOSPEL, "euaggelizo," To bring good news, used in the Old Testament for all sorts of good news, the joyous news of the bounty of God, and above all messianic blessings. (On-line Bible)

Alas, what have we done with this good news? How many times I have felt really uncomfortable hearing people preach to the unconverted a gospel full of accusations and threats! How many times have I heard, "Don't you know that those doing such things have no share in the Kingdom of God? Don't fool yourselves. Those who live immoral lives, who are idol worshippers, adulterers or homosexuals—will have no share in his kingdom. Neither will thieves or greedy people, drunkards, slanderers or robbers." (1 Corinthians 6:10)

Don't you know that? Well, neither do they and contrary to what we often think, it is not up to us to tell them!

Several years ago a friend of mine, Claude Payan, wrote this song:

> *Don't tell him how black her sin is*
> *Don't you think that she already knows?*
> *But say to her that God loves her*
> *And that if on the cross*
> *Jesus gave his life*
> *It is for her and for me*

Let's understand that our work is not to convince the unconverted that they are sinners. The Holy Spirit will take charge of that. "And when he has come he will convince the world of its sin and of the availability of Gods' goodness, and of deliverance from judgment." (John 16.8)

Our work is to tell them the good news, the gospel, and I don't think that you can really consider the fact that you will burn in Hell, as good news!

This gospel is the good news that His grace has been poured out before the beginning of the world, by the love of God. "Your name is written in the book of life, God loves you!" Because in fact, everyone's is…

PREDESTINED FOR HIS GRACE!

People who interpret the Calvinist notion of predestination would be led to believe that evangelism served no purpose, since some have been called to salvation and would therefore be saved, and others would not be! This is incorrect.

Would a good God like ours be able to predestine some people to be saved and others to be lost for eternity?

Certainly not! The bible tells us that God's wish is that none should be lost. "Just so, it is not my Father's will that even one of these little ones should perish." (Matthew 18:14)

No, it is definitely incompatible with the character of our God. The bible describes it like this. Slow to anger, rich in bounty, full of mercy…

How would He be able to decide which of his children burn in the flames of Hell?

Talking of Hell, the lake of fire, the end for sinners, has God created this to torment his children? No, the bible clearly tells us for whom he had initially planned it. "Away with you, you cursed ones, into the eternal fire prepared for the devil and his demons." (Matthew 25:41)

Let's take an obvious example to illustrate this point, the case of Judas Iscariot.

Had God considered this man when he was in his mother's womb as someone who would betray Jesus? This would mean that God had created him to do evil.

This therefore brings us to another question. Our God who is "three times holy," could he conceive and do evil, injustice, treason, corruption, iniquity, greed, theft, which were in the heart of Judas?

After having betrayed the Lord, didn't Judas have the choice to repent and re-enter into God's grace? Evidently he did! He had the choice to do so and be saved!

Sadly, for him, he was trapped by the Devil, even after the Holy Spirit convinced him of sin. Rather than repent and move into grace, he preferred to carry out justice himself, to condemn himself and to execute himself.

Was it God's plan that he should finish up this way?

No. Didn't Jesus continue to call him "my friend" as Judas was in the process of betraying him? According to the verse, "Jesus said, 'My friend, go ahead and do what you have come for.' Then the others grabbed him." (Matthew 26.50)

I guarantee that there was nothing hypocritical in what the Lord said and he truly continued to love Judas as his friend.

Similarly, Peter was no better than Judas because the bible tells us that he renounced Christ three times. "He began to curse and swear, 'I don't even know this fellow you are talking about,' he said." (Mark 14.71)

This signifies that Peter, the friend of Jesus, put himself with those who insulted Jesus and accused him in order to convince them that he was not one of the disciples.

After hearing the cock crow three times, Peter, convinced of his sin by the Holy Spirit, repented and started over again, in the grace of God.

One betrayed Jesus with a kiss, the other insulted him "to save his own skin." But God didn't want to lose either of them and therefore he had not predestined one of them for grace and the other for Hell! What we often take for God's premeditation is in fact a manifestation of the divine attribute, omniscience. Judas wasn't programmed for sin and to damnation. Right up until the last moment he had the choice to refuse to betray Christ and even afterwards he had the choice to repent.

We must understand that God is eternal. This concept of eternity is difficult for us to understand. We live for the moment in a temporary body and therefore, with a chronological view of time. This means that we often confuse eternity with a time which lasts and lasts. But, eternity is the absence of the notion of time.

Yesterday, today, and tomorrow are words which have no value to God. He demonstrated this when he declared to Moses in Exodus 3:14: "I AM WHO I AM. Therefore, here is what you will say to the Israelites 'I AM has sent me to you'." Or, when Jesus himself faced his arrest, "he said to them, 'I AM,' They moved back and fell to the ground." (John 18:6)

This absence of time means that everything that constitutes the story, that is, "the history," of humanity, is laid out before God.

What we call "the prophetic" is therefore not a capacity of divination from God, but is the interface between his omniscience and our temporary reality. That's why the Old Testament prophets were called clairvoyant, or "seers." They did not guess the future. They saw a portion of eternity. God had therefore seen, from eternity, that Judas would betray Jesus. He even announced it!

But God was certainly not the instigator of this betrayal.

Again, we find this principle of omniscience clearly stated, "For those God foreknew, he also predestined to be conformed to the likeness of his Son." (Romans 8:29)

The term that has been translated in English by "foreknew," is "proginosko." "Pro" is the prefix of the notion of anteriority; and "ginosko" translates as the verb, "to know." We are therefore able to understand this verse like this: "GOD KNOWS IN ADVANCE THAT WE WOULD BE CONVERTED." So He predestined us to be like his Son, victor over Satan! Paul says, "What can we ever say to such wonderful things as these? If God is on our side, who can ever be against us? Since he did not spare even his own Son for us, but gave him up for us all, won't he surely give us everything else?" (Romans 8:31)

Knowing the fact that God has not predestined anyone for Hell, proves the love that He has for us all. He does not want to lose any one of us. "God, our Savior, who longs for all to be saved and understand this truth." (1 Timothy 2:3-4)

This is why he had planned, before the fall, the means of bringing his grace and with that, he had planned everything that would follow on from his grace. We can read that "the King shall say to those at his right, 'Come, blessed of my Father, into the Kingdom prepared for you from the foundation of the world'." (Matthew 25:34)

God has loved us from the foundation of the world, and from the foundation of the world he has planned a kingdom for us to take possession of.

The blessing of God is therefore not dependent on whether I deserve it or not, it is simply the grace of God. God doesn't love me for what I do, since He loved me before I existed! He therefore loves me for what I am.

I cannot change a thing, in that I am predestined to be loved by God. The only thing that cannot be changed in my destiny, is the love that God has for me. Understanding that brings us back to posing an important question, which we must discuss.

BEFORE THE THRONE OF GRACE
Or before the throne of good works?

When I present myself to God, am I before the throne of grace or the throne of good works? To answer this question, consider some examples.

<u>First case: I've had a great week!</u>

Sunday morning the pastor gives a message on the blessing of God and you say to yourself, "I've had a great week in faith, I brought my neighbor to the Lord. I read four chapters of the bible every day and prayed for one hour every morning. I made a gift of my car to a brother. Surely the blessing is for me!"

If this sounds like you, then you are before the throne of good works.

Hebrews 6:1 pertains to this discussion. "Let us stop going over the same old ground again and again, always teaching those first lessons about Christ. Let us go on instead to other things and become mature in our understanding, as strong Christians ought to be. Surely we don't need to speak further about the foolishness of trying to be saved by being good, or about the necessity of faith in God."

It is important to note here, that Paul considered the renouncement of good works as fundamental to Christian faith. He exhorted his readers to become mature and not to keep going back to these fundamental points. Nothing that we ever do makes us any worthier of the love of God than we already are.

<u>Second case: I passed the whole week without being near God.</u>

Sunday morning, the pastor gives a message on the blessing of God, and you say to yourself, "I passed the whole week without being near God. I did the same sin again and again, ten times over. I spent my tithe… but I've a whole file of reasons why I had no choice, by a combination of unlucky circumstances I've been sinning but I intend to plead my case. Perhaps the blessing is for me!"

If this is you then you are before the same throne of good works. In fact, by pleading your cause you are in front of the tribunal where judgment is given. The effect of the grace that Jesus has given us is to erase the act of accusation that Satan wants to bring us. If there is no accusation, then there is no judgment.

When we decide to plead our cause, we take ourselves away from the grace of God. He does not want our pleading to reactivate the act of accusation that God has already rubbed out with the blood of the Lamb.

It's a bit like in the book of Acts, when Paul appealed to Caesar. King Agrippa said, "This man could have been freed if he had not appealed to Caesar." (Acts 26:32)

Let's not come before God with human justice. "It's not my fault." is the most foolish excuse that we can use to oppose God's justice. If it's not our fault, then this implies that it's God's fault.

This reminds me of the story of a brother who often ended up in bed with young girls from nightclubs. One day he said, "Lord, if you don't want men to pick up girls, you shouldn't have made them so beautiful!"

God has made us a promise that He will not allow the Devil to tempt us beyond what we can take. (1 Corinthians 10:13)

But remember this—the wrong desires that come into your life aren't anything new and different. Many others have faced exactly the same problems as you, before you. And no temptation is irresistible. You can trust God to keep the temptation from becoming so strong that you can't stand up against it, for he has promised this and will do what he says. He will show you how to escape temptation's power so that you can bear up patiently against it.

If we sin, therefore, don't say that it is your circumstances, because that implies that God has not fulfilled his part of the contract. That would make him out to be a liar!

"It's the Devils fault," you might say. Well, leave it, where it is, at the feet of Jesus, and by the same token, at yours too, conquered and humiliated by the power of Christ.

Understand that whatever happens, the Devil is there to tempt us. He tempted Jesus, and he will do the same to you. By following the example of Christ, because the same spirit is in you, you can conquer the Devil's clever ways, too.

The only way we have to plead our cause or the cause of others, is to proclaim this truth. Forgiveness is always more important than judgment in God's heart.

If you want to plead your circumstances, you will be once more before the throne of good works.

<u>Third case: I did the same sin again and again, ten times over.</u>

Sunday morning the pastor gives a message on the blessing of God, and you say to yourself, "I passed the whole week without being near God. I sinned the same sin ten times. I spent my tithe… I'm not worthy, surely the blessing can't be for me."

We have seen in this study that nothing will separate us from God's love. (Romans 8:38-39)

For I am convinced that nothing can ever separate us from his love. Death can't and life can't. The angels won't, and all the powers in hell itself cannot keep God's love away. Our fears for today, our worries about tomorrow, or where we are—high above in the sky, or in the deepest ocean—nothing will ever be able to separate us from the love of God demonstrated by our Lord Jesus Christ when he died for us.'

If this text is accurate, it also implies that I have failures that are the fruit of weaknesses in the face of the traps and temptations of the Devil and his demons. I can therefore declare that my failures cannot separate me from God's love manifested in Jesus Christ!

In this case again, I approach the throne of good works more than the throne of grace. Perhaps, I have not truly grasped the difference.

DEAD WORKS

The difference between the Gospel and the religions of the world is found here. The religions of the world give us the formula for approaching distant gods, who, for the most part, don't really worry about us.

The gospel tells us that the Kingdom of God has come to us and that God has freely given us his only Son. We weren't interested in God, it is He who has taken the initiative of salvation.

We aren't the ones responsible, and that is often a tough ordeal for our human ego. We want to be worthy of the things that God has freely given us and for that we are prepared to lose the grace of God!

Paul has already explained that grace is the basis of everything. Let's repeat, "Let us leave the elementary teachings about Christ and go on to maturity, not laying again the foundation of repentance from acts that lead to death, and of faith in God, instruction about baptism, the laying on of hands, the resurrection of the dead and eternal judgment." (Hebrews 6:1)

What would he have written to our churches today, if he were to write to them?

My friends, we must ask the Holy Spirit to help us discern dead works, and to empty our churches of all such things. They clog up our churches and often prevent us from doing God's work.

We must learn to discern what is vile and what is precious, what is spiritual and what is religious. All too often, we see people worn out and buckling under the weight of worthless burdens imposed by their pastors or others responsible for churches, or even by themselves.

How many young converts return to the world because of dubious demands put upon them when they join a church?

Maybe you think I'm going too far? Then read what Paul said to the Galatians: "It is for freedom that Christ has set us free. Stand firm then, and do not be burdened again by a yoke of slavery. Mark my words! I, Paul, tell you that if you let yourself be circumcised, Christ will be of no value to you at all. Again I declare to every man who lets himself be circumcised that he is required to obey the whole law. You who are trying to be justified by law have been alienated from Christ, you have fallen away from Grace." (Gal. 5:14)

Reading these verses, we understand that many things will become useless and dangerous in our way of tackling God. These laws we have established and these walls we have built up.

We must watch our old clichés because these can close the church doors to a great number of people who should be there to receive blessing and salvation.

The need to stereotype the believer, in his manner, in his tastes, in his gifts, has made the church a dead place and void of love. We must not become like the Pharisees, whom Jesus compared to tombs: beautiful outside (it's all relative…), and rotten on the inside.

God didn't come to depersonalize us. On the contrary, His aim is that we should find our true personalities, those with which we were created. Who are we to bring into question the quality of

God's creation? And yet, this is what we do when we try to mold the lives of new converts to our principles. How many times have we declared that things that annoy us in others are "sinful," in order to justify our resentments?

Therefore, don't impose useless burdens on converts. "You must do this, you can't do that, you must dress this way, you can't dress like that..."

When I came to church for the first time, it only took a few days before someone had made me cut my hair, take out my earring, detach my jeans from my boots... The people who stripped me of my personality were mainly dressed in three piece suits, which certainly made them look respectable... like mafia hit men! But no more glorious than my fringed hippie shirt! Recall Peter's words, "And now are you going to correct God by burdening the Gentiles with a yoke that neither we nor our fathers were able to bare?" (Acts 15:10)

Several years ago, I was in England for a church tour and I received the following prophecy during a pastors meeting where we were praying for revival in their town, Southampton. This word really shook the spiritual ground for me and made me go back and look again at some of my legalistic convictions.

"I anointed servants to dig wells in the desert. They have worked zealously day after day, sometimes in joy but often in tears, until they found water. This is the water of life of the Spirit. But when they found it, they built a church around each well and the thirsty people for whom I destined the water, were no longer able to get to it.

"Then see, there will come a time when the stones that you used to build the churches will be used to build aqueducts to bring water to the people for whom I destined the water. You will no longer be the guardians of the wells, but of the canals which dispense the water of life to all my creation."

To lack the holy fear of God does not mean to come before Him as a sinner, but to prevent sinners having access to him. We are making an obstruction between God and these people by making a religious program or other man-made convictions. We thus turn those away from Him, who came to save them! It is then that one must have the Fear of God.

GET BACK UP...
After your failures

One afternoon, after having rested, David got up and went to walk on the roof-top terrace of the palace. From there, he saw a woman bathing. She was very beautiful. He sought information about her and was told, "It is Bathsheba, the daughter of Eliam, and the wife of Uriah the Hittite." She came to him, he slept with her and she became pregnant. She sent word to David. Straight away David sent the following order to general Joab, "Send me Uriah the Hittite." Then he said to him, "Go home and rest." Uriah left the palace and the king sent him a gift. But Uriah didn't go home, he went to sleep in the company of soldiers of the royal guard, near the entrance to the palace. The next morning, David wrote a letter to Joab, concerning Uriah. David had written, "Place Uriah in the front line, where the fight is at its most violent, then leave him alone to face the enemy, and be killed." When Bathsheba learned that her husband was dead, she went into mourning. When the time of grieving had passed, David married her and she gave birth to a son. But David had displeased the Lord. The Lord sent the prophet Nathan to him. And, this is what the Lord declares, the God of Israel, "Why have you despised me in doing what is evil in my eyes? You assassinated Uriah, the Hittite. Then you took his wife and married her." David answered "I have sinned against the Lord." Nathan replied, "You are not going to die, but the fact that you offended the Lord means that your newborn child will die."

David pleaded with the Lord in the child's favor. He fasted and went to his house and spent the night lying on the ground. On the seventh day, the child died.

So David got up, washed, put on lotions and changed his clothes. Then he went to the house of the Lord and worshipped. Afterwards, he went home and at his request they served him food and he ate.

David consoled his wife, Bathsheba, and spent the night with her. She gave birth to a son, they called him Solomon. The Lord loved him.

This is an extract from Second Samuel.

I am sure that, like me, you have read the story of David and Bathsheba and that, like me, you asked yourself how a man after God's heart could stumble, and fall into such a sordid experience?

Any court of law would have condemned David to death, or at least to life imprisonment! Maybe not for adultery but, at least, for the premeditated murder he commanded! However, not only did God forgive him, but the Lord blessed David and Bathsheba, and their offspring, even to the point that they figure in the genealogy of Christ! (Matt. 1)

It seems important to me to pick out from this text, not the fall of this great king, but the way in which King David gets up after the fall!

A servant of God is not a man who never stumbles. In no way is he perfect. A real man of God is gauged by his capacity to get back up again after his failures!

When the devil tempts you and seeks to make you stumble, his aim isn't the sin in itself! He knows very well that all sins, past and future, are washed in the blood of Jesus, for those who believe in the grace acquired at the cross! No, Satan's aim is different! He only seeks one thing, and that is to stop you in the calling that God has placed on your life!

God did not change His mind about the calling He had placed on David's life and, therefore, we should think twice before condemning those servants of God who fall. Let us not forget that we shall be judged with the same measure that we judge others! If God does not change His mind about their calling, why do we refuse to allow those who have fallen, to get back up and reintegrate their service for God?

Next, for the person who has fallen, it is imperative that he look upon the situation from a constructive angle, so that he does not abandon the plan of God for his life!

What would have become of Israel if the hero, Joshua, had turned back as a result of his defeat before the city of A? (Joshua 7)

What would have happened if David, the great king, covered in guilt, had slid into depression and abandoned the throne? (2 Sam. 11)

What would have happened if Elijah, after having conquered the prophets of Baal, but then fled into the desert when faced with Jezebel, had not started again in his walk with God" (1 Kings 19)

What if Peter, after his semi-failure of aquatic walking, had gone home to take up the fishing business again? (Matt. 14)

What losses would there be, if Paul, when faced with the interrogations of the Jews and the doubt thrown upon his apostleship, had decided to open a camp site instead of being inspired to write so much of the New Testament scriptures? (1 Cor. 9)

All of the above knew failure, but got up again! Don't play the devil's game, because if you don't get up again, he will have won!

OUTSIDE HIS PLAN…
No blessings?

I am convinced that God has a marvelous plan for every one of us, and I am even more convinced that the best place for every single person in the world is to be perfectly in his plan. I have preached that for many years, and I continue to do so. Yet, I would now like to tackle a reflection that has come back to me several times in recent months. If we are saved by grace, and this salvation cancels the curses which our sinning leads to, are we able to be blessed, and at the same time live all our everyday life outside God's plan? Must we deserve the blessing?

If that is the case, this signifies that a part of our salvation is conditioned by our efforts! This does not agree with the definition of grace given by Paul in Galatians, "Christ is useless to you if you are counting on clearing your debt to God by keeping those laws; you are lost from Gods' grace." (Galatians 5:4)

I got the response to this question in October 2000, when I was in an inextricable situation entangled in my "efforts." We were only ten days away from the start of the "Indian Ocean Souffle Nouveau (New Breath) Convention," when officials of the center that we had intended to use for the event had withdrawn the contract at the last minute. It was a mess and we were looking for marquees, lodgings, transport. I was literally exhausted when the Lord said to me, "Go into the mountains. Pray, fast, and pass the time with me." How would I be able to abandon everything? We didn't yet have any solutions to the many problems and in ten days' time everyone would come. How could I let the rest of the team deal with this situation, while I disappeared up a mountain? To me it felt like madness.

But on reflection, I realized how little time I had given to God during the last few months. I was so busy making a great convention for Him. I decided to respond to His call, and so I left for the mountains and stayed in a small house, to pray and to fast. From that moment, I felt that God would give me instructions as to the solutions for the convention but instead, God had a solution to give me for my life.

After several hours, I felt that God was saying to me "I've missed you, son. Where have you been all this time?" I confess that I did not dare to respond to this question. No excuse would be acceptable. God reminded me of a time in my life when, after many troubles and many spiritual battles, I had decided to leave the ministry.

Cathy and I had completed a course at a biblical training school, after which I decided not to continue to follow God's plan, but those of man's. This action drove me into depression and my sole wish at that time was to disappear and to become anonymous in a church, while building a "professional future."

During the previous several years, I had become a social worker, specializing in the prevention of delinquency. I had always had short term contracts, which never allowed me to stabilize my personal circumstances. So, here we are, in the middle of summer, immediately after having taken the decision to no longer serve God full time. I was offered a post as Assistant Director in a Youth and Culture Centre. It was the position that I had always dreamed of and, of course, I accepted immediately. Three months later, I resigned from this job in order to follow God's plan. I left Savoie for Toulon, France, where I would serve God full time.

Over the years I've thought about this, and I had come to the conclusion that this post was a ruse by the Devil to prevent me from serving God. It was on this subject that God spoke to me at this time in the mountains. "It was I who gave you the job. You had decided not to re-enter the ministry, but that changed nothing about the love that I have for you. I decided to give you your heart's desire because I love you." I understood that God does not try to manipulate us by giving us a false choice between serving Him and being blessed, and not serving him and being not (or less) blessed.

The first thing that I understood during this time is that God is less interested in what I do than in who I am.

He paid a great price, His only Son, in order to be able to spend time with us and in order to bless us like his true children. This is the principle of adoption.

This adoption principle involves some key points.

One must entirely adopt a son or daughter, in a way which makes them of equal status to the adopter's natural children, co-inheritor. (Rom 8:17)

There is no guarantee of love being returned by the one who is adopted, because it is an act freely undertaken to benefit the person being adopted. (Romans 5:8)

But God showed his great love for us by sending Christ to die for us while we were still sinners. How much more will he do for us now that he has declared us not guilty? Now he will save us from all God's wrath to come.

If God has adopted us, it is because he ardently desires to have a loving relationship with us and, in his eyes, nothing is more important than the relationship that you maintain with Him.

At the same time, isn't it true that those who do the will of God will inherit the kingdom? "Not all who sound religious are really godly people. They may refer to me as "Lord" but still won't get to heaven. For the decisive question is whether they obey my father in heaven." (Matthew 7:21)

If we want to understand exactly what it means, 'to do the will of God," it is essential to put this text into the light of the whole of Matthew Chapter 7. To start, note that in numerous translations of the bible, chapter 7 is given this title: "The true religion, Don't condemn your neighbor!"

We can look again at several verses of chapter 7:

"Don't criticise then you won't be criticised. For others will treat you as you treat them."

"Ask and you will be given what you ask for. Seek and you will find. Knock and the door will be opened."

"And if you hardhearted, sinful men know how to give good gifts to your children, won't your father in heaven even more certainly give good gifts to those who ask him for them?"

"Do for others what you want them to do for you."

"Beware of false teachers who come disguised as harmless sheep, but are wolves and will tear you apart."

"All who listen to my instructions and follow them are wise, like a man who builds his house on solid rock."

To do the will of God does not mean the accumulation of things or deeds done in His name. We see how Jesus responded to those who were working to establish his kingdom on a foundation other than the foundation that God had established, the foundation of grace. "I do not know you!" From that we should learn how to recognize and denounce false prophets, as Paul did, in order that the "wolves" do not devour the sheep that the Lord called by his grace.

We can therefore conclude that to do God's will, means to walk in his grace in our personal life now, as much as in the life to come.

THE STUMBLING BLOCK!
What is it?

Surely, you could say to me, "you who are spiritual, your freedom should not become an opportunity for the weak to fall."

How many times have we heard people declare that because of preaching grace, Christians finish up by no longer being sanctified? If this is true, it is because we haven't preached grace but the flesh.

It is easy to conceive that today the flesh is a powerful idol often important in the lives of many Christians. Paul put it this way in his epistle to the Galatians "Brothers, you have been called to freedom, but don't let this freedom become an excuse to live according to the flesh. Be servants for one another in love. The law is summed up in a single commandment, Love your neighbor as yourself."

So we see again that the liberty that Christ offers us is only limited by the love that we give to others.

I must therefore become the servant of others in order that they may discover this liberty themselves.

But generally, it is to others, to those who are ignorant, to the weak, to young converts that we generally refuse Christ's liberty. It is in this way we that we become a way for them to fall, not because of our liberty, but because of our chains!

It is, for the most part, our desire to control which pushes us to renounce the marvelous message of grace in people's lives. Too often we have chosen to walk in front, in the spotlight.

We are God's servants. We are the elders. We are men Women, submit to us). We are the parents. We are those who have been converted for a long time, and we are convinced that to exercise the authority of our position gives us the right to judge the lives of others. Your hair is too long. He's not the husband for you. You must be stricter with your children. And all this is generally presented with the rational because the bible says so!

But when someone takes an in-depth look at the word of God, they can also say that the bible says we declare patronizingly that our freedom should not be a cause for the weaker amongst us to stumble. The only thing that freedom should cause to fall is the authoritarianism of some people over the lives of God's people.

Too often we've manipulated people with the verse concerning the stumbling block and the freedom, putting them as diametrically opposed.

We should understand, that Jesus himself has been in certain circumstances, the stumbling block! "Even his disciples said, 'This is very hard to understand. Who can tell what he means?' Jesus knew within himself that his disciples were complaining and said to them, 'Does this offend you? Then what will you think if you see me, the Messiah, return to heaven again? Only the Holy spirit gives eternal life. Those born only once with physical birth, will never receive this gift. But now I have told you how to get this true spiritual life. But some of you don't believe me.' (For Jesus knew from the beginning who didn't believe and knew the one who would betray him). And he remarked, that is 'what I meant when I said no one can come to me unless the father attracts him to me.' At this point many of his disciples turned away and deserted him. Then Jesus turned to the Twelve and asked, 'Are you going too?'

Simon Peter replied, 'Master, to whom shall we go? You alone have the words that give eternal life'." (John 6:60-68)

Because he spoke truthfully, Jesus caused people to withdraw from him. They abandoned Christ and were therefore lost because of Jesus.

Someone might say to you that your long hair (like mine), your earring (like mine), could be a stumbling block for someone who is weak in his faith. What if I am not going to change my look. So? These things have a tendency to shock embittered Christians. Apparently, some let such things stop them from being able to advance in the things of God, more so than many young converts, who are assumed to be weak in their faith, but who often bring more souls to Christ than those who judge them because of their looks or appearance.

LIVING STONES
Or uniform bricks?

Jesus does not use bricks that are all the same, one on top of another, to build his church, but He uses living stones. Have you ever seen two identical stones in nature? Certainly not! They are all different and that is why God's creation is so beautiful.

When you construct a building from natural stone, you don't stucco or paint it because you don't want to hide the beautiful, uniquely individual stones under a coat of ugly gray cement or synthetic colors! You would only use a topical covering to mask plain concrete blocks, all of which are identical and easily put in place, but hardly very beautiful!

It is the same thing with a church. When it is built with Christians who are "living stones," it is harder to build. It needs more work because you need to find out which stone fits with another; you need to take the time to clean each stone and show the best of it. You need to secure each one according to it's function with each of the others, to imagine the finished result not from a single stone, but from what it will look like as part of the whole construction.

Whereas, when one constructs with Christian "gray concrete blocks," all the same, the construction is much faster, but one needs to quickly apply a rendering coat of religiosity!

Another thing that characterises concrete block construction is that it is particularly economical in it's use of cement. The surfaces are flat and less mortar is sufficient to hold it all together. With natural stones you need a lot more cement mortar.

In the church, this cement is the love that we must give to one another. If we wish to economise on love, are we really busy living God's kingdom, "He who has loved the world so much?"

When all this construction work is finished, our wall will be a marvellous sight because of the beauty of it's stones. It will become a work of art. The church, the bride of Christ, is then worthy of his king.

Too many pastors want to build too quickly, to crush the life of the stones that God has entrusted to them, in their brick mold.

But we must, as Christ did before us, be ready to be a stumbling block for those who prefer religious law to the life of the spirit.

SO, WHY DID GOD CREATE THE LAW?

The law has its role to play in our salvation. It is to make us aware of our sinful state. It is in giving us contact with the law that the Holy Spirit makes us understand when something is not quite right in our life, and to make us aware that we have been separated from God. In making us understand this, a reflex for spiritual survival leads us to the cross. Only someone who knows that he is in danger is going to cry help! The law is there so that we know that we need help and to show us that that help can be found in God. But as we've said before, it is for the Holy Spirit to manifest the law and convince the sinner, it's not our job!

That said, God has planned that we should not live by the law, but by grace.

There was a rule (a law) in antiquity which said that if a woman was sterile then she could authorize one of her servants to sleep with her husband—until the servant became pregnant. Then that servant would deliver the newborn while sitting on her mistress' knees, and the mistress would become the official mother of the child. This law represented legality, that is, what was considered "right'." In putting this into practice, Sarah and Abraham were doing nothing contrary to the law. However, this "legal" practice led them into a fair amount of torment!

God said to Abraham that he would give his grace to Sarah, and that she would give birth to a son. Isaac, the child of grace that God had chosen, was not able to live with Ishmael, the child of the law. After a time, God told Abraham to send away the son of the law. Of course, this caused Abraham, as Ishmael's father, sorrow. Sorrow in giving up his son and sorrow because legally Ishmael would have been his posterity. But, Abraham obeyed his God.

In the same way, we must stop giving birth to "Ishmaels," which we then tearfully send away.

It is never easy to abandon the "little rules" which we have fixed, which we consider to have come from God. After all, we have applied ourselves to do "the 'right' thing."

And yet, we must abandon these legalisms and "right" practices if we don't want to fall from grace.

"…It is written that Abraham had two sons, one from his slave wife and one from his freeborn wife. There was nothing unusual about the birth of the slave wife's baby. But the baby of the freeborn wife was born only after God had especially promised he would come." (Galatians 4:22-31)

Now this true story is an illustration of Gods' way of helping people. One way was by giving them his laws to obey. He did this on Mount Sinai, when he gave the ten Commandments to Moses. Mount Sinai, by the way, is called Mount Hagar by the Arabs— and in my illustration Abraham's slave wife, Hagar, represents Jerusalem, the mother city of the Jews, the centre of that system of trying to please God by trying to obey commandments and the Jews, who try to follow that system are his slave children. But our mother city is the heavenly Jerusalem, and she is not a slave to Jewish laws.

That's what Isaiah meant when he prophesied, "Now you can rejoice, O childless woman; you can shout with joy though you never before had a child. For I am going to give you many children—more children than the slave wife has."

You and I dear brothers, are the children that God promised, just as Isaac was. And so we who are born of the Holy Spirit are persecuted now by those who want us to keep the Jewish laws, just as Isaac the child of promise was persecuted by Ishmael the slave wife's son.

But the Scriptures say that God told Abraham to send away the slave wife and her son, for the slave wife's son could not inherit Abraham's home and lands along with the free woman's son. Dear brothers, we are not slave children, obligated to the Jewish laws, but children of the free woman, acceptable to God because of our faith.'

Does that mean ...

LIVING WITHOUT LAW?

Let us read Galatians, "Brothers, you have been called to freedom, but don't let this freedom become an excuse to live according to the flesh. Be servants for one another in love. The law is summed up in a single commandment, Love your neighbor as yourself. If you keep on biting and devouring one another, watch out or you will be destroyed by each other. So I say, live by the Spirit, and you will not gratify the desires of the sinful nature. For the sinful nature desires what is contrary to the Spirit and the Spirit what is contrary to the sinful nature. They are in conflict with each other, so that you do not do what you want. But if you are led by the Spirit, you are not under the law." (Galatians 5:13–18)

The first thing we should take notice of, from the text is "the law is summed up in a single commandment, Love your neighbor as yourself."

Often, we start by trying to accomplish the law the wrong way. Because, for example, it seems easier for us not to kill and not to steal. Some make superhuman efforts not to commit adultery. But, we always leave loving our neighbor until last and loving our enemies, for another time!

The problem would resolve itself if we started doing as Paul told us—by loving our neighbor. I am unlikely to steal from someone I love, nor kill them, nor run off with their wife.

Don't look for this kind of love inside yourself, in your soul or feelings, since you won't find it there. This kind of love is a fruit of the spirit, mentioned in Galatians 5:22. Therefore, look in your spirit. In fact, no man will ever find in himself the capacity to love, with the love that God defines in 1 Corinthians 13. "Love is patient, love is kind and envies no one, it does not boast, it is not proud, it is not rude, self-seeking, not easily angered, keeps no record of wrongs. Love does not delight in evil but rejoices in the truth. It always protects, trusts, hopes and preservers. Love never fails."

Having said that however, we must keep searching for this love in the presence of our God, in order for it to be able to be manifest in ourselves. We need to be permanently connected to this source of love in order to be able to spread it around. My experience is that the more time I spend with God, the more I am able to love others.

The second thing that we can learn from this text is the fact that God gives us the key to living not under the law, that is to say, to not being driven or led by the flesh.

This key, once again, calls on His grace rather than our strength, "Be led by the Spirit!" Again, this demands humility from us.

HUMILITY IN SANCTIFICATION

The Lord tells us in Proverbs 29:23 that, "A man's pride brings him low, but a man of lowly spirit gains honor."

The Bible teaches us that we must be humble and, with this humility, we are able to have access to glory. For this, we must learn to appreciate the joy of our successes rather than glorifying ourselves from them.

It often occurs to me that when I have been able to resist temptation, it wasn't because I had been such a "good Christian," but because God had stopped me from falling. Also, I have regularly found that if I don't give God all the glory when I have success in my ministry, in the following days, I fall back into sins, long since abandoned.

Some years ago, I zealously wrote a list of everything that I had given up for God. It gave me a certain pride. I didn't particularly display it, but I remember that it gave me more than just a healthy feeling of satisfaction.

My attitude with regard to other Christians changed. I thought that since I was having victory in certain areas of my life, I was in a position to give advice to others around me. If the principle of others profiting from our experience is a good one, it must be in a spirit of love. In the weeks that followed, I fell back into certain weaknesses.

I realized that God often made his grace available to me to stop me from falling, and it was more His victory than mine. The Lord's Prayer takes on a new significance for me now, "Don't let us fall into temptation."

Our role, in our sanctification, is to keep our eyes fixed on Christ and to reside in His grace, and give glory to Him.

INVITATION TO THE GRACE PARTY

It is interesting to note that every time God gets his people together it's to have a party. We can read this in Leviticus 23, "here are the feast days of the Lord, which you are to proclaim as sacred assemblies, The Lord's Passover begins at twilight on the fourteenth day of the first month. On the fifteenth day of that month the Lord's Feast of Unleavened Bread begins, for seven days you must eat bread without yeast. Here are the feast days of the Lord, which you are to proclaim as sacred assemblies, for bringing burnt offerings, sacrifices, and drink offerings required for each day."

We can see again that God considers Jerusalem as a party town. "Look at Zion, the city of our festivals!" (Isaiah 33:20)

Jeremiah laments that God's festivals are no longer celebrated. "The roads to Zion mourn for no-one comes to her appointed feasts. (Lamentations 1:4)

Then God promises, through Nahum, that the times of the Messiah will bring back the parties to the middle of the people. "Look, there on the mountains, the feet of one who brings good news, who proclaims peace, celebrate your festivals O Judah, and fulfill your vows." (Nahum 1:15)

I believe that for almost 2000 years, the messenger of peace, the Lord Jesus, has been with us to announce his peace. He also came to ask us to celebrate a new Passover, i.e his sacrifice on the cross.

For my part, I am an admirer of the communion. Not only because it reminds us of the expiatory sacrifice of Jesus Christ, without which we would not have access to the grace of God, but above all because it gives us the assurance that I can present myself before the Fathers' throne, without any inhibitions, because Jesus has gone there before me.

The Communion, my friends, is the most marvellous party to which we could ever be invited. It is the anti-chamber to the heavens. I often say, jokingly, that it is the "aperitive" before the wedding of the Lamb.

In our worship, Communion happens in the middle of the time of praise and adoration because that's what motivates us.

Personally I would like to go to church and see nothing in the worship but the following three things:

- Communion
- Praise and adoration
- Tithes and offerings

In our local church we often worship this way because we consider that the meeting should be entirely turned towards God. In traditional worship, where the word from the pastor is the heart of the proceedings and intended for the parishioners, it seems to me that the Christians benefit more from the praise than God does!

Certainly this implies that the people of the church are faithful to the meeting where the word of God is preached, so as to feed and at the same time become disciples.

Again I repeat, religions say that we need to give worship to a god in order to become one of the saved. But we do it because we are saved.

It is important that we understand what the bible tells us about Communion and for that, we must read what Paul says in the epistle to the Corinthians. "For what I have received from the Lord, I pass on to you. The Lord Jesus, on the night he was betrayed, took bread, and when he had given thanks, he broke it saying 'This is my body which is for you, do this in remembrance of me.' In the same way, after supper he took the cup, saying, 'This is my blood of the new covenant, do this whenever you drink it, in remembrance of me.' For whenever you eat this bread and drink this cup, you proclaim the Lord's death until he comes. Therefore, whoever eats the bread or drinks the cup of the Lord in an unworthy manner will be guilty of sinning against the body and blood of the Lord. A man ought to examine himself before eating or drinking, for anyone who does so without recognising the body of the Lord eats and drinks judgment on himself. That is why many among you are weak and sick, and a number of you have fallen asleep. But if we judged ourselves we would not come under judgment. When we are judged by the Lord, we are being disciplined so that we will not be condemned with the world."

Looking at this text, we can answer a major question: what does it mean...

DRINK THE LORD'S CUP IN AN UNWORTHY MANNER?

The aim of the Communion is to remind us of the most essential thing about Jesus' time on earth. This is neither his teaching, nor the miracles that he did, it is the redemptive sacrifice that he offered and freely gave on the cross, for ALL who believe.

Paul therefore warns us to be on guard of the danger of being scornful of those for whom salvation is addressed, when we ourselves benefit from it. Paul tells us in this text, "for anyone who does so without recognizing the body of the Lord eats and drinks judgment on himself."

Yet the body of the Lord is made up of all those who are and have believed! Without exception! Paul says to us here that if there are sick people, and deaths, it is because certain people think they are capable of discerning better than God himself who is part or not of the body of Christ. Paul reminds us here of the old adage of the speck of dust and the plank. If we judge ourselves, then we won't be judged.

Remember that the context of this letter that Paul was sending to the Corinthians was division.

He started with a greeting explaining that we are saved by our faith in Jesus Christ, and that that implies that we belong to him and that from now on we are called to live FOR HIM in being members of his body "To the church of God, at Corinth, to those who are called to live for God and belong to him, by faith in Jesus Christ..."

He continues his greeting and blessing to all those who believe in Christ, whatever their local church at Corinth declaring that his Lord and theirs were one. "...and all those who wherever they are, call upon the Lord Jesus Christ, their Lord and ours. May God the father and the Lord Jesus Christ give you grace and peace."

Paul then made this urgent call, "Brothers, I appeal to you in the name of Jesus Christ our Lord, that all of you agree with one another so that there may be no divisions among you and that you may be perfectly united in mind and thought."

He declared that our goal is to belong to the body of Christ, and never to any old denomination! Paul continues: "one of you says 'I follow Paul', another 'I follow Apollos,' another 'I follow Cephas,' still another 'I follow Christ'."

Finally, he clearly announces that the body of Christ cannot be divided! "Is Christ divided? Was Paul crucified for you? Were you baptised into the name of Paul?"

We often spend too much time discussing the errors of others rather than witnessing love and respect to them as brothers in Christ.

"Then you will call, and the Lord will answer; you will cry for help and he will say, 'Here am I.' If you do away with the yoke of oppression, with the pointing finger, and malicious talk, and if you spend yourselves on behalf of the hungry, and satisfy the needs of the oppressed, then your light will rise in the darkness, and your night will become like noonday." (Isaiah 58:9-10)

God doesn't want us to engage in making fun of others or nasty behavior, even to our brothers who are in the wrong. On the contrary he wants us to witness to his love as much by what we say as what we do. Then our darkness will be as bright as the midday sun.

How many times, my friend, has this disappeared from our view? How many times have we missed the target (this is the definition of the word "sin") from firing left, right and centre at anything that moves, that is not in our limited comprehension of God's plan? How many times have we forgotten to love?

I simply wish to be lucid, here. We must confess our sin to God, since this is what it is, and to ask him to change our mentality. Thus, it is not believing that the Bread stays as bread and the Wine as wine, not blood, which is going to make us ill! Nor even the fact of taking the communion in a state of sin, which risks killing us! In that case, we would all be dead and buried!

But the fact that we don't discern the body of Christ around us, in others, and so not giving them the love and attention that we owe them.

Our hearts are too small for us to be able to love like God loves us. Love our enemies, those who hate us, those who persecute us, those who don't follow the same doctrine as us etc. This is not the domain of our soul but of our spirit. We need to realize that not one of us can manifest a fruit of the Spirit from his soul!

Then how can we have Christ's feelings? How can we make this commandment a reality, day by day? Christ got there because, HE WAS NOT DOCTRINOCENTRIC!

I have sometimes, and perhaps you too, had the impression of not being worth any more than the Pharisees who reproached Jesus for healing on the Sabbath. We want to be the valiant defenders of the doctrine and we speak of theological purity, forgetting that the "logic" of the "theos" is the LOVE that surpasses all other considerations.

So that this love will become a reality we must consider others to be of equal, if not greater importance than ourselves in God's plan. This is possible if we keep our eyes fixed on Christ, more than on ourselves. We are truly able to discern the BODY.

BAPTISED INTO A SINGLE BODY

"He did not say this on his own, but as high priest that year he prophesied that Jesus would die for the Jewish nation, and not only for that nation but also for the scattered children of God, to bring them together and make them one." (John 11:51-52)

We can see in this text that God's plan is to bring each of us, who were isolated before meeting Christ, into a single body with Jesus at the head. During our first steps in the faith, we find ourselves immersed (baptized) in God's people. I remember that at my conversion, I had the feeling of having literally dived into a new world full of people who loved me. At this time, I didn't want to hide anything at all from my new family. I wanted to be part of it all and wanted all the barriers to fall. I wanted to become one with them all.

Now reading Romans, we can define a basic rule for the functioning of the body. We need each other to function. "Just as each of us has one body with many members, and these members do not all have the same function, so in Christ we who are many form one body, and each member belongs to all the others." (Romans 12:4-5)

We must not allow ourselves to take this lightly. Take the example of the car. We find different pieces inside. The ignition key, the sparkplug, the bolts to securely hold the spare wheel, etc. You can't start the car with the sparkplug, or change a flat tire with an ignition key! That's why one needs all the correct tools to undertake a safe journey.

A Christian cannot live without the rest of the body. A Christian cannot blossom alone. And in the same way there will always be something missing in a meeting if other Christians are regularly absent.

Too many churches think that they are able to do without a part of the body of Christ! My friends, in heaven there will not be any Pentecostals, or Baptists, or Catholics, or Protestants or Anglicans etc. There will only be the people saved by the blood of Christ. This blood, like the blood in our physical bodies, circulates through all parts of the body without exception! Certainly each part is different and we don't for a minute want the hands to be the feet or for the heart to do the work of the stomach. We can and must have different functions because God has created these differences for us to spread evangelism into the maximum number of lives. Each of us matches to particular characteristics of the population but all must obey the same order of Jesus to make disciples of all the nations.

This baptism into a sole body is the only thing of importance at the moment of taking the bread and the wine. It is absurd to think that only those baptised in water have the right to come the Lord's table. For a start, there is no biblical foundation to back up this theory, also this gives baptism a significance that it does not have.

BAPTISM IN WATER

There are always many questions about the subject of baptism. Some people see it as a sort of act which is more or less magic, others as a condition of salvation. It is neither one nor the other. 1 Peter 1:9 tells us "you are receiving the goal of your faith, the salvation of your souls."

There is nothing else that is able to give it to us. If we make baptism a rule, then we no longer walk in God's grace: "I do not set aside the grace of God, for if righteousness could be gained through the law, Christ died for nothing."

Baptism is something for the saved and only for them. Philip says to the eunuch in Acts 8:37, "If you believe with all your heart (which means that you are saved, as the act of believing brings salvation) that it is possible." The eunuch replied: "I believe that Jesus Christ is the son of God. (that is to say, I am saved)."

It is clear that during the calls to conversion that is recounted in the book of Acts, Peter did not ask anyone to bow their head, and even less to raise their hands. And this is what he said to those who asked, what they needed to do to be saved. "Repent, and be baptized in the name of Jesus Christ." (Acts 2:38)

Baptism is therefore not a grade which we attain and which brings us new prerogatives in the church. It is therefore not necessary to be baptized to take communion.

SECOND PART

GRACE THE SUPERCHARGER OF FAITH!

Or how to live by faith…in grace.

When we truly understand what God's grace is all about, we must walk in faith to take hold of this grace. We must understand that faith and grace are inseparable because they are two faces of the same coin.

First of all, note that faith is received by grace. "Simon Peter, a servant and apostle of Jesus Christ, to those who through the righteousness of our God and Savior Jesus Christ have received a faith as precious as ours." (2 Peter 1:1)

We have received FAITH, by justice (THE GRACE) of God! Afterwards it is up to us to turn this gift to good account until we can take, by faith, all that is God's grace.

It's a bit like the pin code on your bank card. To start with you receive your card and your pin code; then, when you want to withdraw some money, you put your card into the machine and tap in your code. God has given you a card for the bank of his grace, with which you can draw on the inexhaustible resources of God's love. With the card comes your own pin code and the code he has given you is… F-A-I-T-H

You cannot disassociate one from the other. You need the revelation of grace to understand that it is not your good works that give you access to God's blessing, but your faith in his grace.

How many people, who truly have faith in God have nevertheless never really understood the fact that God wants to bless them.

We often hear things like this: "If God wanted to heal me, surely he could… Lord, if it is your will that I want for nothing then you will provide… When God wants me to prosper then he will do it…"

This type of remark gives us doubts about the essential point: God's desire to bless us. We will look at this in detail a little later, but understand that one of the fundamental principles for obtaining grace, your banker card, is useless without the pin code!

"It is by grace that you are saved, by faith, and this is a gift from God." (Ephesians 2:8)

As we read in this text, we see that we are saved by grace but faith is the means. If I do not have the means, then grace does not work.

God doesn't throw his grace to us, he holds it towards us!

This means that we must take it. Grace is how God acts to benefit us, faith is how we act to take this blessing.

In Galatians we read, "Christ redeemed us from the curse of the law by becoming a curse for us, for it is written "Cursed is everyone who is hung on a tree." He redeemed us in order that the blessing given to Abraham might come to the Gentiles through Jesus Christ, so that by faith we might receive the promise of the

Spirit." (Galatians 3:13-14)

The Greek term translated here by 'to receive' is "lambano" which means, amongst other things, to take with the hand, to grab hold of a person or an object, to take what is yours, to take over yourself, to reclaim, to procure, to fight to obtain, to take something owed.

Here we have a translation much more active than that given by the word receive. This more active translation seems much more in line with our daily life experience. We can reread the text as "...and we seize by faith the Spirit that was promised."

How many amongst us have faithfully awaited God's blessing without receiving it! We end up believing that God does not want to bless us for various reasons and we end up at the throne of good works. "When I become more holy, when I pray more, when I witness more…"

But the reality is something else. We see people doing less than us and being blessed more, simply because their relationship to God's blessing is not passive, they seize God's promises and hold them tightly!

God offers his hand full of blessings towards us for us to take by faith.

We have long ago debased the term "to live by faith." Many people think that this means to sit patiently by and wait for God to act.

"To live by faith" does not mean to wait for a hypothetical blessing, but to act with the faith that we proclaim! Because this faith is based on the fact that God has chosen to give us his grace. To put it another way, God is good, so act accordingly!

We find the word "grace" in the old testament which in Hebrew is "kheh'-sed" which translates in the bible as bounty, mercy, fidelity, love, and grace.

We see that grace is the true nature of God. And he offers us this grace! It's up to us to take it for ourselves.

Afterwards we can see the magnitude of this grace in Romans. "For if by one man's trespass, death reigned, how much more will those who receive (SEIZE) God's abundant provision of grace and of the gift of righteousness reign in life through one man, Jesus Christ." (Romans 5:17)

This grace is abundant, God does not offer us just a little bit, but an abundant grace. The bible teaches us that GOD IS RICH IN BOUNTY! RICH IN GRACE! Through grace he wants us not to be slaves, but on the contrary, to be those who reign! It means that we must, if we want to reign in life, seize the abundance of his grace.

PERSECUTED BY HIS GRACE!

We are not here at the beginning for nothing. God, in his love, is ready to persecute us with his grace.

Reading the Psalm 23:6, "Surely goodness and love will follow me, all the days of my life." There again, the Hebrew term translated by "to follow" is much stronger than our English equivalent. In fact, "radaph" in Hebrew, can also mean to chase, to persecute, to harass! My friends, God's grace will chase you and it will persecute you until you take hold of it!

It seems important to me, at this point in our study to wring the neck of an old doctrine which has driven God's people to live outside his grace because of a misunderstood verse.

"To keep me from becoming conceited because of these surpassingly great revelations, there was given me a thorn in my flesh, a messenger from Satan, to torment me. Three times I pleaded with the Lord to take it away from me. But he said to me: My grace is sufficient for you, for my power is made perfect in weakness. Therefore I will boast all the more gladly about my weaknesses, so that Christ's power may rest on me." (2 Corinthians 12:7-9)

To start with, we must accept that this splinter does not come from God as some people sometimes maintain. It is clearly stated that it comes from one of Satan's angels!

Further, it is important to consider the definition of the word sufficient. In Greek arkeo (arkew) which can be translated as "to possess an inexhaustible force."

It seems therefore that Paul was facing a problem that seemed to him to be impossible to resolve. Why?

Perhaps Paul had tried to sort it out himself. Had he perhaps in this battle, believed that his position as God's servant sheltered him from this kind of problem and perhaps he went before the throne of good works, "Lord, see how I serve you well. It's not fair after all that I've done for you over the years, you could have helped me avoid this." We have seen earlier that God wants us to approach him with a humble heart.

But he gives us more grace, that is why the Scripture says "God opposes the proud but gives grace to the humble." (James 4:6)

One thing is certain, it had brought him to failure, since he had prayed several times without result. These are perhaps the failures which made him realise he had nothing to boast of and to believe that he could do anything without God's grace.

Nothing indicates however that Paul was stuck with this problem to the end of his days! This certainly does not correspond with the character of our God, full of grace!

Once the lesson has been understood, it seems that God reminded him of the key to the vault of our faith.

MY GRACE IS INEXHAUSTIBLE TO SOLVE ALL YOUR PROBLEMS

This angel of Satan has already been vanquished by my grace manifested in Jesus Christ. You are the beneficiary of this grace. Take hold of this power now.

We are a long way from what we often hear. "Suffer in silence and be content with your salvation. You will not go to Hell, it's all OK, but while you're waiting don't ask for too much!"

This kind of thinking comes about because the fact that many people have a greatly reduced vision of the significance of the word "salvation." This word comes from the Greek "soteria" which has a number of meanings:
- Deliver from an enemy.
- To heal physically.
- To heal spiritually.

God, when he sent us his salvation, didn't just send us a promise of resurrection in the future. He sent us resurrection immediately. "When you were dead in your sins and in the uncircumcision of your sinful nature, God made you alive with Christ; He forgave us all our sins." (Col 2:13)

He gave us life, in the full sense of the word! This includes the three parts of our life, body, soul and spirit. The grace of God also operates therefore in these three domains.

By this grace we will be able to enter into our land of Canaan.

So what projects does God have for us ?

A LAND FLOWING
WITH MILK AND HONEY

One Sunday, during the worship, as God's spirit was leading us to sing in tongues, I received a vision from the Lord:

I saw dozens of poorly dressed people on a hill gathering bitter herbs. that they were putting into wicker baskets. They were all Christians. It seemed as if they were about to live through a long and difficult food shortage.

I sensed the presence of Jesus at my side. He had his arms full of brightly-colored fruits, wonderfully-smelling bread, pots full of honey and drinks of marvelous colors. All these things were not only nourishing, they were evidently succulent.

The people approached the Lord but they were not taking all the good things that he was offering them. I was surprised by this but then the Holy Spirit showed me why. The people had the habit of nourishing themselves with bitter herbs, not wanting to waste their time taking God's blessing. They were unable to truly understand that all these things were in fact intended for them.

During the week after this vision, I asked myself how these people, of which I was part, were able to be content with this misery as God's children whilst they had the right to seize God's promises!

But did they truly know these promises and did they know that they were intended for them? No, just like me, they had no idea what God has for them.

"Say to them, this is what the Sovereign LORD says, 'On the day I chose Israel, I swore with uplifted hand to the descendants of the house of Jacob and revealed myself to them in Egypt. With uplifted hand I said to them, 'I am the LORD your God.' On that day I swore to them that I would bring them out of Egypt into a land I had searched out for them, a land flowing with milk and honey, the most beautiful of all lands'." (Ezekiel 20:5-6)

Firstly, we are not predestined by God to eat bitter herbs all of our life! God wants us to live in the most beautiful of all lands, there where milk and honey flow. He tells us in His Word that He has sought this land for us! He made the effort to give us the best!

But what is a country flowing with milk and honey? The response seems clear, it is a country where we want for nothing. If even such luxuries as milk and honey are provided in abundance, how much more so the necessities of life. God's plan for our lives is that we want for nothing, neither necessities, nor luxuries! This is the normal attitude of a father towards his children.

We must, from now on, let go of the idea that God would want to hurt us.

Jesus teaches us the following, "Which of you fathers, if your son asks for a fish, will give him a snake instead? Or if he asks for an egg, a scorpion? If you then though you are evil, know how to give good gifts to your children, how much more will your father in heaven give the Holy Spirit to those who ask him." (Luke 11:11-13)

I asked myself, when reading this text, why Jesus put the accent on the Holy Spirit, as the basic gift that God gave to his children, on the same level as a human father gives his family food to eat. This is because it is the Holy Spirit who gives us the certainty of our status as God's children.

"Those who are led by the Spirit of God are sons of God. For you did not receive a spirit that makes you a slave again to fear, but you received the Spirit of sonship. And by him we cry 'Abba, Father.' The Spirit himself testifies with our spirit that we are God's children. Now if we are children then we are heirs, heirs of God and co-heirs with Christ, if indeed we share in his sufferings in order that we may also share in his glory." (Rom 8:14-17)

Why, in fact, do we expect anything from God if we don't have the certainty that He is our Father! Only this profound conviction could lead us to have the same trust towards our heavenly Father as a child towards his earthly father.

Alas, this is the problem. In our modern society, the example our parents give us is not the same as in Jesus' time. In the western world, many fathers have given up on the education of their children, the affection towards them and sometimes even their material needs. How many men and women come to Christ with a bad opinion of the paternal role, transferring their frustration in this domain onto God.

Some people think that God only blesses in a spiritual way. Has God changed, then, since the time of Abraham? Has the blessing of God been all used up?

THE LORD BLESSED ABRAHAM ... IN ALL THINGS.

This blessing of Abraham consists of several words "Abraham was old, advanced in years; and the LORD blessed Abraham in all things."

God blessed Abraham in ALL THINGS! And today, he wants to bless each Christian in ALL THINGS! He wants us to be satisfied in our years, fulfilled with riches, fulfilled in affection. He simply wants our happiness.

In Genesis 39:3 we read, "His master saw that the LORD was with him, and that the LORD gave him success in everything he did."

The same as in the beginning of 3 John 1, "Dear friend, I pray that you may enjoy good health and that all may go well with you, even as your soul is getting along well."

God wants all to go well with us, in every aspect of our life. He established the human being as three parts: body, soul and spirit. Since God created us this way, we can therefore expect the Lord to make us prosper in these three domains: material things for the body, affection and intellect for the soul and anointing, that is to say, a portion of Holy Spirit resting upon us, for our spirit.

People accept more easily the fact that God blesses spiritually, than physically. Several verses in Deuteronomy show us the Lord as far from "having his head in the clouds" when it comes to blessing us. Your bread basket will be blessed, "The LORD will command the blessing to be upon your storehouses and in all your undertakings... He will bless the country that the LORD your God has given you... The LORD will send you treasure, the heavens, the rain in his timing, to bless all the work of your hands; you will lend to many nations, and borrow no more... The LORD will give you victory over your enemies, who rise up against you; they will go out against you by a single road, but will flee before you by seven roads."

Alleluia! All these promises are still the will of God for us today!

How can I know the will of God for us, you might ask? By following the same reasoning as Paul. If God loved us so much he gave the most precious thing he had, his only son, there is no reason why he would not give us so much more. Let's read together Romans 8:32, "He who did not spare his own son, but gave him up for us all, how will he not also, along with him, graciously give us all things?"

IF WE SUFFER WITH HIM?

What, then, does the end of this verse mean?
"Now if we are children then we are heirs, heirs of God and co-heirs with Christ, if indeed we share in his sufferings in order that we may also share in his glory." (Romans 8:17)

Are we expected to suffer the same sufferings as Jesus, to be "crucified," in some way, in order to be adopted?

We have just seen that this is not the case. Do our children deserve to be loved, or do we love them because they are our children?

God loved us so much that he gave us his only son to save us from the curse of the law that man is under.

In Galatians 3:13 the apostle Paul tells us, "Christ redeemed us from the curse of the law by becoming a curse for us, for it is written 'Cursed is everyone who is hung on a tree.' He redeemed us in order that the blessing given to Abraham might come to the Gentiles through Jesus Christ, so that by faith we might receive the promise of the Spirit."

The curse upon the people of God because of their failure to obey the law has been taken away by Jesus on the cross. He became the curse, even though he has fulfilled all of the law, in order to give us a new, and higher, covenant by his blood. We no longer have to personally merit Abraham's blessing, as Christ has merited it for us. We only have to seize it, as we do our salvation, by faith!

However, the fact that we seize our salvation freely from Christ and the blessings that go with it, put us automatically into a position of being an enemy of Satan.

How many friends turned away from me when I became a Christian? How many members of my family mocked me? How many things that I used to enjoy have I had to abandon to follow Christ? These are the sufferings Paul is referring to.

But, my friends, what you abandon is nothing in comparison to what God will give you!

For that, we need to change our regard, and have...

EYES OF FAITH

"And the LORD said to Samuel, 'Do not consider his appearance or his height, for I have rejected him.' The LORD does not look at the things man looks at. Man looks at the outward appearance, but the LORD looks at the heart."

I have often heard, and even used to think, that faith is not seeing problems. Alas, when faced with facts, I could only think that I was simply not a man of faith.

A servant of God, who was praying for my ankle, broken twice in ten months, declared to me: "Your ankle is completely healed! Do you believe it?"

My reply was: "I believe that God can do it, but I can see that my ankle is still broken!"

This was a dilemma for me, for years. I finished up by thinking people mad for declaring "by faith" that they were healed when they were visibly not. However, I felt I was missing something important. This continued until I realised that God was neither mad, nor blind, in the domain of faith.

I understood that I had been mistaken, in reading this verse. In fact, God does not say that he does not see our weaknesses or capacities, or the situations. He says that he does not look at them! "Man looks at what is eye catching, but the Lord looks at the heart."

What is the difference, you might ask? To see is a passive verb, what is around me, but to look is a premeditated action that I control.

In other words, we are not responsible for what we see, but we master what we look at, and so take responsibility over our reactions.

If you had seen me 15 years ago, you would have seen a young Christian, perturbed, violent, proud, and rebellious.

But alleluia! Others saw me with different eyes. They were willing to "look" at what was hidden from men, and "look" further, to see what God wanted to make me into. They had eyes of faith. In the first years of my conversion, lots of things were not sorted out in my life. In particular, my inward healing, and therefore the regard that I had towards others. One day, when my first son was born, and I did not have any work, I played the guitar in the streets to earn a living. The leader at the church I had started going to, suddenly passed by. I felt embarrassed as he slid a bank note into my guitar case, and invited me for a coffee in a cafe, nearby. He said to me: "I didn't know that you play the guitar. You should come to church Tuesday, and play in the worship group with me."

At this moment, I took my packet of cigarettes, and lit one. Rudely, I blew the smoke in his face, and replied, "And now, do you still want me to bring the guitar?"

To my great surprise, he said "yes." For the first time in my life, someone looked at what I was going to become in Christ, instead of seeing just the exterior.

If today I am in the ministry it is mostly due to this anecdote and this brother, to whom I will always be grateful.

In deciding to abandon what we see to look for what God wants to do, we enter into the domain of the miraculous!!

Literally for me, the result was obvious. I saw my ankle, deformed by numerous operations, but I decided to look at what the word of God proclaims, "He himself bore our sins in his body on the tree, so that we might die to sins and live for righteousness; by his wounds you have been healed." (1 Peter 2:24)

The result of this attitude wasn't long in coming. Since that day, I have walked miles and miles in the bush to announce the gospel in far-flung villages in Madagascar! Praise God!

My friends, this is nothing to do with positive thinking which says: "I am not ill, I am not ill, I am not ill," when I am in agony. Faith is declaring "I am ill, but I am healed by Jesus' wounds!"

The difference between the two seems small, but it is a gulf that separates faith capable of producing a miracle, and the pale imitation that Satan attempts to give to lead people into hell.

This principle applies to all aspects of our life as we have already seen.

FAITH BIG AS A MUSTARD SEED

"Lord have mercy on my son, he has seizures and is suffering greatly. He often falls into the fire and water. I brought him to your disciples but they could not heal him.

"O unbelieving and perverse generation, Jesus replied, how long shall I stay with you, how long shall I put up with you? Bring the boy here to me. Jesus rebuked the demon and it came out of the boy, and he was healed from that moment.

"Then the disciples came to Jesus in private and asked 'Why couldn't we drive it out?' He replied: 'Because you have so little faith. I tell you the truth, if you have faith as small as a mustard seed, you can say to this mountain, 'Move from here to there,' and it will move. Nothing will be impossible for you'." (Matt. 17:15–21)

I have sometimes heard teachers say that faith as big as a mustard seed suffices to get rid of the mountains in our life and to do big miracles.

Most of the time, these teachers make me uncomfortable. I used to think that my faith wasn't even the size of a microscopic mustard seed, and thus led me into feelings of guilt, depression, rebellion or even abandon. If after all I had seen God accomplish in my life, my faith wasn't even that big, it was obviously because I wasn't worth much.

This was a burden, not from God, that hindered my spiritual growth.

My friends, if you have experienced this, or are doing so at the moment, I have very good news for you. In no way did Jesus mean that only a small faith could move mountains, but reproached his disciples regularly for their "small faith." Jesus tells us rather to take example from the immense faith of a mustard seed.

Imagine the faith of this seed. The smallest, according to the word of God (Mark 4:31) of all seeds! Despite that, it will become the biggest of all plants!

This tiny seed must, for that, have a large faith. When it is planted, it is crushed, and buried. We try to drown it with water. Then there is the hard earth, so difficult to pierce. As soon as the plant puts its first feelers outside, the sun is there to burn it, a storm comes along and breaks its leaves, and the animals who try to eat it. This seed discovers ten, a hundred, a thousand times that the circumstances are against it! But despite this, it continues to grow, and one day, birds will nest in its branches.

Jesus wanted to show us the immensity of faith, not the smallness of a mustard seed. We could say that deep down, inscribed in the genetic code, God has promised this seed "I created you to be the biggest plant in the garden!" Our little seed doesn't look at the circumstances that try to go against the plan of God. It only looks at the promise inscribed deep down: GOD CREATED ME WITH A PRECISE GOAL, I WILL ACHIEVE THIS GOAL!"

This is faith, a faith which grows despite the circumstances. Understanding these things, we read this text differently, "in truth I tell you, if you have a faith that doesn't look at the circumstances, you could say to the mountain."

Friends, reading these lines, your faith is not smaller than that of a mustard seed! Maybe it hasn't yet reached the maturity to believe despite the circumstances, but this will come. Don't be discouraged.

Your faith has saved you, this is a miracle when we understand what has gone before.

I BELIEVE...

Come and help me in my incredulity!

"Jesus said: 'If you can, everything is possible for him who believes.' Straight away the father of the child cried, 'I believe! Come and help me in my unbelief!'" (Mark 9:23-24)

Satan confronts us with situations that our faith hasn't been prepared for. He seeks in this way to lead us into failure.

But God, in his desire to bless us, doesn't leave us disarmed before it. He knows our capacities and when they are limited, he sends us a spiritual gift of faith. This is what Jesus does for the child's father. He comes to help his faith, so that the miracle will happen. This figures in the list of spiritual gifts as given in 1 Cor. 12:4-9.

"There are different kinds of gifts but the same Spirit. There are different kinds of service but the same Lord. There are different kinds of working, but the same God works all of them in all men. Now to each one the manifestation of the Spirit is given for the common good. To one there is given the message of wisdom, another the message of knowledge by the same Spirit, to another faith, to another gifts of healing." (1 Cor. 12:4-9.)

There again, we are confronted with the inexhaustible grace of God which demands us to have faith, but which comes to our rescue when ours fails, as it does when temptation becomes too strong for us to resist.

"No temptation has seized you, except what is common to man, and God is faithful, he will not let you be tempted beyond what you can bear. But when you are tempted, he will also provide a way out so that you can stand up under it." (1 Cor. 10:13)

LET ME FLY...

In conclusion, let me tell you a story of a farmer who wanted to adopt an eagle. He thought that the best way was to find a nest and take an egg home for one of his hens to warm. The eagle, brought up in the courtyard would thus be domesticated. He put his project into action, and several weeks later, a chick eagle was strutting around amongst hens and ducks.

Though he grew and soon overtook the size of the other birds on the farm, our domesticated eagle went here and there, scratching the ground, and never trying to take off and fly.

Oh, he had certainly noticed that his wings were longer than his friends' and it was a handicap for him in everyday life. He didn't have webbed feet either, so efficient for swimming in the duck pond! The only time he tried to go in the water, he nearly drowned!

What a silly eagle, mused the farmer, a little disappointed to see the regal bird scraping the dust like a vulgar chicken!

And yet, one morning, whilst the courtyard was busy, a piercing cry resounded. The old hens, used to recognizing dangers, quickly went for shelter in the shed, hen houses and other hiding holes, followed promptly by the other animals. And soon, only the young eagle was left in the courtyard.

The cry made him look up and he saw a huge bird, which seemed to frighten all his friends at the farm. The cry, though, didn't scare him at all. He tried to call out, and found that the same sound came from his beak.

So, blinded by the sun that he had never taken the time to look at before, so busy scratching the ground, he stretched his unused wings. He beat and beat and beat, so well that he was soon in the air. What a wonderful sensation, to be able to fly like the huge bird whose cry sounded like his. So much like... like a father. He never returned to the farm, as he had finally understood why he had been created.

"You have seen what I did to Egypt and how I carried you on eagles' wings and brought you to myself." (Exodus 19:4)